Lying Mirrors

Lying Mirrors

An Encouraging & Thought Provoking Read

Carter M. Head

Heads Up Publications
Atlanta

All rights reserved. No part of this book may be reproduced or transmitted in any form or by any means, electronic or mechanical, including photocopying, recording or any information storage and retrieval system without written permission of the author except for brief quotations used in reviews, written specifically for inclusion in a newspaper, blog, magazine, or academic paper.

Scripture quotations marked (KJV) are from the King James Version of the Bible.

Lying Mirrors
Copyright © 2017 by Carter M. Head
Published by Heads Up Publications
Book Cover Illustrator: MR4GX

ISBN: 978-0-9988323-0-2
Ebook ISBN: 978-0-9988323-1-9
Library of Congress Control Number: 2017937165

Heads Up Publications Books are available at special discounts for bulk purchases for sales or premiums.
Direct all inquiries and correspondence to:
Heads Up Publications
P.O Box 162593
Atlanta, GA 30321
e-mail: headsuppublications@gmail.com

Printed in the United States of America

This book is dedicated to the memory of

Contents

Introduction IX
Foreword XIII
Declaration for the Reader XV

Chapter 1
The Author Personal Accounts 17

Chapter 2
Lying Mirrors 25

Chapter 3
Are there 2 of Me? 33

Chapter 4
When Reflections Communicates 41

Chapter 5
Embracing the Real ME 47

Chapter 6
You are Unique and Wonderfully Made 55

Chapter 7
Unclothe the Façade 61

Chapter 8
Will YOU Allow the Real Me to Come Forth? 71

Chapter 9
Obtaining Oneness within Ourselves 79

Chapter 10
Evolving into the True Essence of Me 85

Chapter 11
Changing Mirrors 93

Chapter 12
Pretending to be Okay 101

Chapter 13
On a Quest to Understand 107

Chapter 14
The Authors Final Answer & Conclusion 115

Consequences of Walking in Lying Mirrors 121

Identity Points..123

Introduction

The motive for the writing of this book is to prompt the reader to discover and acknowledge their true self. The true self can never be offended because there is nothing to offend when one displays themselves to others as grounded and authentic. However, when an individual displays a façade image to others it most likely increases their chance of being offended because they have to convince others of the authenticity of their false identity. The false identity that an individual display has to feed off people perceptions of who they think they should be, therefore they practice evolving into that proclaimed image until it creates into a lying mirror.

The average person projects a lying mirror in which they reflect a façade to others to conform to their world of approved perception in order not to experience rejection. People who do not display the real them, but different mirrors depending on their situation and who they are interacting with are most likely experiencing an identity crisis, not to be confused as a schizophrenic. The question posed in the mind; what do I need to display to be accepted? The question posed in the heart; will they accept me if I reflect the real me? Lying mirrors is a self-help book. Lying mirrors allows people to reflect, evaluate themselves, and pose questions about their behavior, culture, and many other characteristics that have assisted them into conforming to who they currently are. This compendium will inspire readers to begin to discover and accept their real selves and reflect who they are at heart that they may be at peace with displaying one true mirror.

There are many reasons why some people will not tell the truth about their self as in reflecting their real identity to others. Some fear that other people cannot handle their truth, which encourages them to continue to conceal or keep sensitive secrets disclosed. Some fear the result of their exposure, experiencing anxiety due to rejection, ostracization and desecrated by others. Being honest about oneself takes courage, and it makes some people uncomfortable.

Just know that eventually you, I, and maybe many more will begin to accept the truth about ourselves and strive towards perfection towards our true identity. Please do not continue to feel and think negative about yourself because of what other people think about you, no matter what it's time to be free to be you. Results of accomplishing this mindset will help us not to have to continue to present a façade around others and frees us up from those who think they know us, into having a better relationship amongst each other and peace within ourself.

Listen please do not read only a few chapters of this book "Lying Mirrors" read it all and be introduced to the real true essence of all your Identities. But first of all I must have you to know, after reading "Lying Mirrors" you will begin to make decisions' about your life that others will not understand and they will question your intentions. There will also be times when you second guess yourself, but just start the new course of your true identity.

Foreword

The concept of identity crisis has been present in human nature from the very beginning of our existence. The earliest example being Adam; blessed with dominion over the earth as well as the burden of leadership, but ultimately remembered for adversely changing the world as we know it in a moment where he went against his better self. Throughout the course of our lives, most of us have wrestled within ourselves for peace, acceptance, understanding, and ownership of our own identities. Many of us have exerted and wasted excessive efforts in attempts to control what others perceive about us while failing to control what we perceive about ourselves.

This book addresses that dilemma in such a way that will leave the reader feeling enlightened, liberated, and empowered. Enlightened by the insight provided about the inner workings of the mind and how it deals with conflicts within itself. Liberated by the positive affirmations of self-worth and acknowledgement of purpose; finding freedom from all the voices (of others as well as our own) that tell us that we are not good enough, beautiful enough, smart enough, or wealthy enough to be identified as valuable. Become empowered by deeper knowledge of self and better realization of who we are. Think of the many stories we have heard and witnessed of men and women who discovered their real selves and owned what they found - they went on to lead movements, make history, and save lives. We too have those callings and predestinations woven into our fabric by our God. Read on… and let us lay claim to our true and higher selves.

– John F. Dilworth

"There is nothing noble in being superior to your fellow man; true nobility is being superior to your former self."

– Ernest Hemingway

Declaration for the Reader

One of the hardest things for each of us to deal with is bearing the feelings of not being appreciated and honored by people close to us, even the people that have opportunity to be in our presence. This emotional roller-coaster has put us in a mindset of needing validation and likes. This why most of us are hooked on social media sites where we can share many different facades. We long for attention; but I am making a declaration on your behalf.

Today I will cease searching for validation and appreciation from others. I will today start on a quest to stop overlooking me and my challenges. I will face all of my lying mirrors and evaluate who I should not be and who I will eventually become. I declare I am not too busy to become the True Essence of my Being. I miss me, and I will allow the True Image of who I really am to come forth in my mirror.

XVI | Lying Mirrors

"The two most important days of our lives are the day we were born and the day we found out why."

– Mark Twain

The Author Personal Accounts

Be mindful that playing the game of chess within our own mind can cause conflicts of our own multiple personalities some people call their alter egos. We must understand that our multi personalities are in essence our own fingerprints and actually define us as a unique individual with our own minds and thought processes.

The hardest mindset and frustrations I have had to endure was the chess game of defining my true identity through the reality of the many different purposes throughout the course of my life; from as far back as I can remember dating as early as 1st grade when I was in elementary school. You and I had purpose as children and we were being molded into who we would eventually reject and deny, causing us to grow up as unstable, playing a chess game within ourselves.

    While playing the chess game, we were going back and forth, listening to others, mimicking our peers, feeding off impressions of other people whether on television, in movies, on the internet, in our communities, associates in a setting of worship, and especially people viewed as celebrities and sport figures. You know our idols; people we have looked up to as being special and important, people we desired to be like. As I reminisce on my past life events, I recognize that some of the behaviors and thoughts that I promulgated were purposeful then and that those same behaviors and thoughts are molding and prompting me in most cases to be patterned or conformed into the essence of my being in this stage of my life thus far.

    My past life experiences have helped me to recognize the truth about who I really am from the very start. The chess game I had been playing within myself even as a child reflecting on my identity now brings back memories. I remember in grade school that I had a purpose as a peacemaker and unknowingly a counselor. As a child and in my early teens, I would intervene in fights to try to stop the aggression, and the times I was not successful in stopping the fight of my peers after the fight was over, I would console the aggressor and the weaker fighter as I do now as a leader. I also now realize during my early teen years when I enjoyed writing letters, poems, and drawing pictures to post on my bedroom wall; unknowingly these passions were honing into one of my purposes as an author.

    We must cease from feeling guilty of not being or adding up to be who and what others want us to be. I remember in parenting my children, with my first child I had not received a degree in parenting nor had I taken classes on how to be a great parent that makes all the right decisions in reference to encouraging my child to be who she wanted to be in life. Instead, I promulgated the opposite; I had a fixed desire and expectation, also a preconceived notion of what I expected her to do and who I expected her to be.

Be careful that we are not allowing ourselves to be mentally conformed to someone else such as our church doctrinal beliefs or parents and family member's desires; for which they think and perceive us to be from their standpoint; even our idols and mentors lives that we sometimes believe are intriguing. Let us be mindful that we do not have to solidify who we are, based upon the ideologies of others we are prone to follow. What others want you to be may be in conflict with your true self.

Here's an example of what my wife and I experienced from a religious standpoint of how we were operating in a mindset and a traditional doctrinal belief system that we chose to adhere to that was a very religious concept one that neither of us agreed with but we still allowed ourselves to be dictated by. In which a particular church my wife and I attended believed women should not wear pants, makeup, nor jewelry and my wife followed the church protocol even though we did not agree with those standards. My wife and I were in bondage, and the sad thing about it was we thought and even considered that it was okay to adhere to this particular doctrinal belief system.

Approximately two years later an incident occurred that made my wife and I realize that we were living a lie. My wife and I were shopping at a grocery store in proximity this particular church we were attending at that time. As we were checking out at the cash register behind us in line were three people waiting to check out as well. One of the people that were standing in line behind us was the bishop of the church we attended and when my wife noticed the bishop made eye contact with me and her she nearly fainted.

You may ask why did she nearly faint; it was because she had on pants, jewelry, and makeup and our Bishop saw it. After my wife and I entered into our car and rode back to our home we talked about the encounter at the grocery store involving our Bishop. My wife and I knew that a religious lifestyle was not a true reflection of whom we were and that is why we learned at that particular moment that it is important to be comfortable in our own essence. We all must learn to be okay with the essence of who we are. By not allowing others and their ideologies make us or discourage us to the point of us living a lie about who we are just to please them.

Unit Reflection 1

Think back as far as you can remember. Write down the good, the bad, and the ugly life experiences that have had a major influence on developing the current behaviors and present life style you display today. What did you do then that you find your mind thinking now and your actions and responses adhere to now?

Lying Mirrors

Have you ever considered that you may be a pretender? Pretenders do not know how to be themselves because they are busy mirroring someone else's behavior. In a world full of pretenders, we have been embellishing in an identity crisis in which power of persuasion or suggestion has pressured us into the mindset of allowing people to have the power to validate who we are to be. This has been happening so long that others have labeled most of us as being schizophrenic, outcast, religious fanatics, crazy, and even phony. I believe this effect is being promulgated to and in us by subliminal messages, traditions, and worldly concepts; in which develops and enhances in our cellular memory. Sophia Stewart calls it the Matrix.

If we do not awake unto the truth about who we are and take back our ability to make our God-given choices, we will continue to be as other people want us to be and not be who we were put on this earth to be. We are wearing too many hats. It is time to activate the real you, by pursuing the real and true you, so that you may come forth!

Once you make the conscious decision that you want to present to others who you are, when you look at your reflection in the mirror you are most likely to see the scarring that is invisible to everyone else. Your scars may be under the umbrella of fear, hurt, guilt, condemnation, lack, divorce, shame, jealousy, bondage, rejection, addictions, failures, sickness, hate, ignorance, doubt, or any other negative events that you have experienced in your past that are embedded in your heart. In the initial part of facing the negative events that are in your heart, it may cause you to be uncomfortable and unpleasant emotions may come to the surface. Nevertheless, it is beneficial for you to face your issues because it introduces you to self-awareness. You do know, it's past time we stop lying to ourselves. Your freedom starts with you being honest with you.

When we finally have the opportunity to walk in our true self; then and only then can we stretch beyond ourselves with liberty and assurance. We cannot stretch beyond ourselves without frustration once we accept the truth that we are currently someone who we are not supposed to be. Change is uncomfortable, but the truth is if you do not make the effort to change, you will not experience change and ultimately peace and assurance.

Please allow me to acknowledge first; in this book, I am not promulgating schizophrenia, religion or a traditional church doctrine. This book is to assist you in the process of identifying your self-worth from a personal perspective. This book was not written to scare you of the uncertainty of who you could become, but only to progress you into the next chapter of your truthful identity. This book is not the solution; its motive is to encourage you to open up your heart and mind to increase your self-awareness and to walk in the real you because most of us are confused about who we are and supposed to be on this earth.

    I wrote this book to assist in freeing up the minds of the people who are broad and open-minded thinkers that think outside the box and thinkers who want to experience walking in their truthful identity. Our real identity should not be solidified according to our race, culture, religion, environment, mentors, or spiritual experiences. We should not have to be just a representation of the place where we were born and raised or what our early school teachers suggested we were according to the history books, which supposedly solidified where we ranked on a scale of importance. We should be free and at liberty to express ourselves in the true essence of our God given and God purposed beings.

I am not promoting retaliation towards any suggested group or organization that most believe could be involved in a government take over. I do not believe we that are the chosen of God have to be too concerned about anybody or their possible use of witchcraft, persuasion, plots or diabolical plans to interrupt or cause our demise or death; due to their knowledge of us being in opposition and objection towards their methods and mindsets to intimidate us. No fear is my motto. Rest assured in whom we are. For years, people have been trying to fix everybody else and cannot even fix their self.

Oh! I am enthused to allow this book to enlighten you to the truths about who you are because you have always known and had an inclination in your gut that there is a better person inside of you. I have a good feeling about this! Well, here we go! Check this vital information out. Did you know that a neuroscientist by the name of Dr. Michael Gershon was criticized in the medical world when he found and suggested that the human body have two nervous systems? Dr. Gershon stated that one-half of our nervous systems is in our gut, the other half is in our brain and are both joined by the left vagus nerve. The second brain in our gut is the sixth sense, which is the other us. This comes from the saying; "my gut feeling and something told me." Maybe we need to listen more to our gut because our gut do not have to pretend and be someone that it is not. The gut represents liberty after we accept the truth about whatever it tries to share with us. Now do not stop here, read on. We have only scratched the surface of revealing your true identities.

Unit Reflection 2

In what ways do you reflect a lying mirror to others? What are your motives when presenting a lying mirror to those persons?

Are there 2 of Me?

Will the real you come forth? This chapter will enlighten you, the reader, to the most difficult endeavor most of us will ever embark upon and succeed in, as unto expecting and peacefully walking in the true essence of your real identity. Without reserve and without confusion, and I am being very optimistic on your behalf, due to the fact you have made it to this chapter about the "Other You."

Again, let it be known, you must realize there is another you fighting within and against the true essence of your being. This reality will be your final challenge and final victory of coming out of and away from the reflections of the Lying Mirrors. First, by moving past the fear of people not receiving or embracing the real true you. We must get over others not understanding or honoring our true essence and identity. I believe achieving this will not be a problem to overcome.

We must accomplish the most difficult task of overcoming and overriding the main opposer who is the other you. I am referring to the part that is of the mindset of complacency, being comfortable with continuing to walk in false identities that keep you locked into the Lying Mirrors. You and I must fight vigorously against the main opposer; the other you; the pretender, the other you that is keeping us from walking in peace, assurance, and victory within ourselves, knowing that in doing we all will become happier and live an easier life.

The battle of the identity crisis lies within our mindset. We behave one way in secret and around people who we know accept us for who we honestly are. However, when we are amongst other people, we behave in what they consider is the norm because we sense they may ostracize us for presenting to them the real us.

Not as to identify us with the stigma of schizophrenia, in which this term and diagnosis have been discovered to have a negative connotative and was understood to be irreversible because most neuroscientist and psychiatrist labeled this term schizophrenia to mean a mind-split disease. However, in 2002 the Japanese Society of Psychiatry and Neurology changed the term from Seishin - Bunretsu- Byo to Togo- Schitcho- Sho, which is an integration disorder. When schizophrenia began to be viewed as an integration disorder, it leads to the increase in the percentage of cases more than 40% over the first three years in which it became controversial, thus leading to the operational criteria used today when diagnosing people with schizophrenia. You may not be a schizophrenic.

It also became clear after the 1971 US-UK Diagnostic Study that schizophrenia was diagnosed to a far greater extent in the United States of America than in Europe. In which concluded that the diagnosis of schizophrenia in the U.S. was often subjective and unreliable. In the Soviet Union, the term schizophrenia was used for political purposes, to discredit and expeditiously imprison political dissidents. I believe and some would agree that some people that have been associated with the stigma of being schizophrenic have been misdiagnosed.

I know of a man who was labeled dysfunctional and schizophrenic only because of his outspoken values on issues of injustices. He stated, "It was promulgated that I was dysfunctional and schizophrenic; by the mindset of the city and county officials during that time; which was of racial apathy." They painted the picture of him as being a so-called radical and rebellious person;

eventually they influenced him to seek help in a mental institution and he was diagnosed schizophrenic. I believe that after the counselors had interviewed him they labeled him as schizophrenic because he had a different viewpoint on current issues. Most of us are being evaluated by people that cannot figure us out: wrongfully.

Nevertheless, I desire to find the true meaning of me, even through confusion, worldly concepts, my cultural upbringing, my religious beliefs, intellect produced by social media (television, the Internet, self-help books, etc.) enhanced intellect. I need to know me! However, whether you are consciously aware of it or not we are experiencing a dilemma because our brain has absorbed all of this information from some of the sources previously mentioned and it has caused and produced or developed a person inside of a person within ourselves. I have labeled this dilemma as "The 2 of me" and "The other me."

The question asked has been lingering in me, a long time, "Who am I?" Some psychologist calls this psychodrama, which is a dramatic story with psychological overtones originating in the mind as emotional conflict. The base word for psychodrama comes from psychology, which is the science of mind and behavior, the mental and behavioral characteristics of an individual. Joyce Myers wrote a book about it and titled it Battlefield of the Mind.

I, along with many of us, am experiencing this dilemma and I now believe this book is a great insight on how to overcome this dilemma and confusion and begin to be released to walk in our true identities in freedom, liberty, and assurance. Thus promoting us to operate on this earth no matter where we go or whom we are around in peace, victory and with love in our heart towards every human with rest in our soul to enjoy the abundant life that God expresses every day in our midst even in bad situations.

I believe and have come to understand that throughout my career as a manager, business owner, husband, father of four, and pastor for 13 years that I was not ever really of certainty that I was who I was projecting at any given time, situation, or forum in the presence of people. I have always felt okay in my mind that I was doing what was expected of me in a specific genre and while doing it I received accolades for doing it well. However, in my gut feeling I knew that it was more to me in a whole other area of self-worth. I knew it had to be better than this. I now understand it was the other me prompting me to continue to seek my real identity. I come to realize that with this thinking we are not double minded or schizophrenic; but on to something special important and fulfilling that will possibly promote, peace, assurance, joy, happiness, and rest within yourself. Now you really have to read on to see the outline towards your new existence.

Unit Reflection 3

Make a list of the good & bad characteristics that you can identify within yourself. Once you have completed the list, identify the characteristics your associates have disclosed to you, on their perception of you.

When Reflections Communicate

Our reality is a deliberately created illusion similar to what Sophia Stewart shared in the Matrix. This world is false; so who am I? Are we good actors? Could it be that most of us are just experimenting with our identity by playing different characters throughout the course of our life? Obviously, we then are more than likely communicating within ourselves.

Who is behind the tattoos, wigs, weave, colored hair, implants, makeup, provocative clothes, smile, sagging pants, mean expressions, gold teeth, and flashy apparel? Where did we learn to project outer appearance from? Who taught men that having sex with more than one woman solidified their manhood? Where did fornication and adultery come from? Will the real you step forward.

Are we as the Nicolaitans who are make believe pretenders, phony, acting like someone we are not? Why do we think, it is not ok to be ourselves? Is it possible that others are controlling us and manipulating our minds to believe a lie about us? This is called the power of suggestion or the power of persuasion; a method of mind control. We have been convinced to believe we are not good enough and in order for us to be someone else that we think others will appreciate and love. Our need for validation, to feel loved and needed, pulls us towards living a lie. We are perceiving what and who we want to be because of what others prompt us to be. If they hurt us or separate themselves from us, we then at that point allow them to help us feel lonely and rejected; which is not truth. Someone cares for us all.

People also can control us to think like them; this is what magicians influence us to do when they perform magic acts they use the power of persuasion. We need to just be ourselves and think what we want to think about us and handle the scenarios we experience on our own. "How?" you may ask. By not convincing yourself that, everybody is right by you. We are hoping for what others want to see about us and we play into it. Magicians cannot do a trick without another human participating in which they utilize the other person's mind. We must stop agreeing with others that speak negative in reference to who we are.

Allow me to share with you why I continued to pastor at my church for 13 years; it was only because the people I was associated with suggested that they thought I should but within my gut, I did not really desire to, but the people who were in opposition of my ministry wanted me to fail. To prove to the people that I was not a failure I kept pastoring the church. However, on a positive note it is rare that some of us like me have had the privilege to connect with people in a church which enhances and help bring out the real us. As a result, my choice of continuing to pastor the church was not in vain; but it still was not what I desired to do and be at that time in my life.

Listen, the power of persuasion or suggestion is a symbolic process to convince other people to change their attitudes or behaviors regarding an issue through the transmission of a message in an atmosphere of free choice; utilizing words, images, sounds, etc. It is a deliberate attempt to influence others to follow its lead without opposing its influences. Self-persuasion is key in which people are not coerced they are instead free to choose.

Methods of transmitting persuasive messages can occur in a variety of ways including verbally and non-verbally via television, radio, the Internet, or face-to-face communication, even by fear and intimidation, also discrediting measures. The powers of persuasion/suggestion are forms of mind control, therefore, please do not be gullible. Realize and pay attention to who and what is dominating your thoughts. Be careful not to idolize other humans. Remember you are seen as equals in God's sight. Know that no one is better than what is greater within you. So, none of us have to take the backseat to no other human at the cost of discrediting another. Okay by now this book has come alive within your understanding, read more.

Unit Reflection 4

Research the topic of the power of persuasion, suggestion, and influence. Consider the influence that subliminals can have on a person's way of thinking and behavior patterns.

Embracing the Real ME

We must become one within ourselves before we can sincerely unite with others. Being phony is one of the causes of suicidal and high divorce rates. Most of us spend all of our lives struggling to be what others require of us then we die and those same people who we have tried to please; forget all of our efforts. Be careful not to spend the rest of your life appeasing to people that themselves are not sure of their true identity as well.

We must understand; when we begin to experience living in our true identity we will not have to try and convince anyone who we are or who we are not. If you can tolerate being the way you are now you probably will not change. I can only recommend, promote and suggest change its inevitable and we can only accept change when we are uncomfortable with the way we exist. Most of us have to lie to others just to be accepted but lying is not the way, being ourselves and being genuine should be our goal in order to live a peaceful life. Just know, we will always operate in an atmosphere of what we assume is real or maybe it is just illusions (not as it seems).

Perceptual psychology (mental processes we use in everyday living to evaluate each other) can cause us to misinterpret people, situations, and what they represent. We perceive a lot more than we realize through all of our senses. It is like what we see under a microscope; it is not what we see without it. Our brains try to make sense of what we see by using what is already in our senses along with what we do not see. In other words, we finish an unfinished product by using perceptual psychology meaning assumptions.

People typically analyze according to what is already in their brain from subliminal perceptions in their cultures, teachings, traditions, and experiences. That is why people sometimes perceive things differently. The Neuroscientist Jim Baggott researches reality alternate realities with no connects to what is in society, which are fantasies. A shared reality is that all of us believe in money if we did not our economy would collapse. Our realities are created by society; billions of brains working in sync to establish a concept over thousands of years. When people tell stories, are they real? A reality distortion is optimistic, but the reality of the situation to justify us all continues in certain situations.

Our high expectations have to be removed from the things and people that are not working with us on our behalf. Listen, I need you, but I am not trusting in you. I think we put too much trust in each other especially when we do not even trust in the real us. Proof in this is that most of us lie to ourselves and if I am not true to myself, it is obviously evident that I will not be true to you. We must become consciously aware of ourselves in regards to our identity: The 2 of me. We are mind, soul, and spirit. We have to become one within ourselves. I reference to one of my favorite Biblical scriptures, John 17:11 where Yeshua prayed that you and I become one before we can unify with each other.

It has always been the good me versus the bad me. Come on now; there is a side of you that is negative; Neuroscientist say, in a course of 24 hours there are approximately 7000 thoughts that goes through a human brain every day. I do not believe all 7000+ thoughts are good positive thoughts; do you? However, we as a people do not have to contend with these differences but embrace them in order to grow in wisdom. Each of us are being compelled by and through negative and positive events in our lives to do better, to come up with solutions to the problems, also to endure and increase our stamina. As well as having the ability to continue in this life. We have to know, no matter what our circumstances entail or what the outcome is, knowing we are here for a reason, because you are not a mistake or a freak of nature. You are wonderfully made.

Are we out of touch with the real world? Because, negative thoughts can dictate how we see others and even ourselves. Some people brain seems to resist negative information about their self and they tend to think negative more about others. Most people that are not excited about their self tend to enjoy the hurts of others. Maybe one reason why some of our society embellishes in bad news more than good news about others is because those people in particular only wish they could live as good as the others and they are not so when they hear bad news about others they tend to feel gratified in the hopes of another demise. I believe it makes those people feel better about their miserable lives.

Will the real you step forth and prompt the other you to come into an agreement to be one with self! If you are not one with yourself, are you aware of the division inside of you? The negative side of you is possibly the part of you that has conformed to the subliminal messages of this worlds system. You do not have to experience division anymore within yourself; you just have to submit to the true you and be okay presenting the truthful mirror to others no matter who tries to assassinate your character.

Make sure the real you is projected in the mirror because other people are always observing your reflection. You are a living epistle and maybe just maybe people have been judging you by the person you displayed to them which is not the true epistle. Now is the time to listen to your heart, look at what you are reflecting in the mirror and come to the realization which voice you need to begin to yield towards more. We must also compare that voice with morals, truths and love with the concept that God is real and personal in our lives. The confusion within mindsets about us has to cease. We need both of us to survive, grow and learn from our mistakes.

We are in a Matrix, but we will be birthed into the real us. Are you tired of being tired of being who everybody else wants you to be? It cost to be you, the real you because no one else can be you. It is your story and no one knows your whole story. We do not have to pretend anymore to be who other people convinced us to be; we can now enjoy being who we are. We now do not have to receive or believe anymore lies about our true identities. The next chapter will validate you. Thanks for receiving thus far.

Unit Reflection 5

Make a list of what you would change differently about yourself and explain why.

You Are Unique & Wonderfully Made

I am intrigued to realize that it is ok not to be normal: I am referring to the so-called norm that bombards us every day by the projected subliminal messages. A subliminal is inadequate things, pictures, and events that produce a mental awareness. This developing what is called cellular memories are the databases of cells with memory that records everything that has happened to us throughout our existence and stored in our cells, not just in our minds.

A subliminal tends to influence our relationships, thoughts, feelings, emotions, bodies, health, love walk, and perception of life. This could possibly be the reasons why we react towards one another as we do especially from a negative connotative. You may wonder why, it is because we subconsciously need others to validate who we are, this unknowingly becoming enslaved to their ideologies. Is not this bondage to the third degree?

Question: can we go deeper? Well, what if you and I were actually a part of a cloning experiment? Would you really know the real you from the cloned you? We must not only know but also understand our true identity; the one within us, underneath all attributes and traits of cellular memory, subliminal messages, persuasions, suggestions, worldly concepts, traditional and cultural development.

I do not know about you, but I am so uncomfortable and discouraged at times with this mindset of disillusion I have allowed to assist me in dictating my life. I believe we are just now coming into being okay with ourselves being born outside of this worldly concept of norm. What is a normal person and who declared it so? I wonder what and whom they are comparing me and you to? I do not mean to sound religious, but the Holy Bible instructs us in 2 Corinthians 10: verses 12-18 not to compare ourselves with them that commend themselves as being the perfect or successful model for the human race.

Jealousy and the myth of competition hinder some of us from advancing in the real us. We cannot sum up another person's life with one or two incidents. We do not have the mental capacity to comprehend the conclusion or the reason for any one's life. Thus, we sometimes judge others but only according to our learned standards because not one of us is omnipotent, omnipresent, or all knowing. Therefore, who are we? I too ask why other humans are like they are. Who said that any one individual is all the way right and others are wrong. We do not know the total outcome of anybody's being and existence on earth. Who is right? We think we know and we really do not know, in reference to who someone else should be.

We are unique as individuals and wonderfully made in our own God divine purposed. Who is capable of conforming us into their image? I do not have to look like you or be like you. Who define success? Is it possibly the one who met their own goals and tops out on the level of achievements in which they thought they deserved because they compared themselves to someone else in their line of work discovers success? But not us, this standard should not dictate who we are to be.

Our thoughts are not someone else's thoughts; our goals of achievement should not derive from another's measure of success. Just think about it; making others smile or instilling hope in them could possibly be your God given purpose: the real you. This is success, when we can help just one person experience life with joy and this new you will be in a place of fulfillment and even enthusiastic to go further.

Many of you are already successful in what you have set your minds and effort towards. Success is the prominence actual attempt in doing what you have moved forward in doing. Our identity lies not in the thoughts of others solidifying us and measuring us with the standard of their traditions. No one can merit another's courage, faith, substance, or even strengths based on the subliminals that make up cellular memory. What declares another is better than another? We are all works undone, but seeking to be better and progressing in that goal. With this mindset, I am realizing the truth of what Joel Osteen quoted "You were not created to be unhappy to keep everybody else happy. You've got to run your own race." And you will after you finish reading this book "Lying Mirrors." By now you see that you are eccentric. So do not stop reading. Read on.

Unit Reflection 6

Create a composition (poem, song, literature, or art) that will express why you know you are unique and wonderfully made and what you can change in your life so that others can observe a better reflection of you.

Unclothe the Façade

We are responsible for our own actions we follow certain rules but we are free to make choices within those boundaries and when we go outside of conformities; we then suffer the effect from others by doing so. Stop allowing them to take choice from us, making decision for us, and dictating who they want us to be because if you choose not to stop, you will continue to live a lie. Remember not everyone will accept or understand your decisions and desires.

In order to be free, more of us have to be brave enough to break bondages and consciously know who we are. Society puts limits on our free will. Do we understand the world around us? Yes, I do believe we need a controlled environment as in a way of life on earth. I believe we need a controlled environment only because not all of us will submit to who we really are and thus being controlled by what we were taught which may include negative attributes such as hatred, racism, or jealousy to name a few.

Ask yourself is who you are now tearing you down or building you up? We are being corrupted and God is enlightening us to reinvent. It is time to activate the real and true you that is inside of you. Let us also desire to look at people as Yeshua looks at us; knowing there is love in everyone.

Who made you that way? Who is producing and inventing you? How many have we reproduced from our mode and mindsets? Humans invent raciest, haters, gluttony, disobedience, liars, religious folk, cults, traditions, selflessness, ignorance etc.

Is who you are now contributing to the demise of humanity and catering to frustrations on earth or maybe you are walking in your purpose of promoting hope, joy, peace, and life. The true you, will be free of condemnation, frustration, guilt, and self-doubt by realizing you are an intricate part of solving the problem that is causing the frustration. Frustration and even weariness in well doing comes to us when we desire and need others. We must be free of trusting in others to do good to us. We must be the person promoting and presenting positive attributes to others. Look into our own hearts, see what inflicts us with pain, and remember not to do it to anyone else. Do unto others, as you will others to do unto you.

Let us stop questioning our self-worth or preeminence based upon others. You are special in your own right regardless of who speaks different. We do not have to hate ourselves, just allow the real you to come forth and be the best you that can be. Only you can be you and now is the time to be the best you that you can possibly be. Do not be upset or frustrated because of people rejecting and overlooking you it may be possibly because you have not presented the real you to them as of yet. Frustration and even depression most likely comes upon us when others do not honor, acknowledge, or realize that we are an important and significant gifted individual with worth. I believe when they begin to sense, hear, and observe the true side of you (the good side) they will honor you, as a gift and people will invest in you, in which they will assist the real you to continue to flourish. Because most of us have for a long time been playing games with ourselves: a chess match.

We must stop letting our good deeds be spoken evil of because of the bad vs. good manifesting: We must humble ourselves, be real with ourselves, and stop making decisions from the voice of our emotions and tiredness. Stay calm, thankful, and appreciative in all things. Have you noticed that it always eventually works itself out? Please stop allowing yourself to believe others can fix you. Who said they are fixed?

Life starts with the real me! Life is an adventure when you express it with love. There is a before and after picture of you. All life evolves, age, grow, and progress even by processing and time; it is inevitable we do change eventually. Let us address the dilemma of changing; in order to have peace with our evolving into a position and being aware of a possible opportunity for God to reinvent us into whom we are supposed to be by His design. I am not promoting not liking yourself in the now. I am promoting a change for a more better and fulfilled life full of peace, joy, hope, and compassion because of us operating in the life God defined for us. We do understand God is love and God is good. God is also divine in mercy, truth, forgiveness, and grace.

Coming to our true selves sometimes means we have to let go of the plan we had for our lives in order for God plan to manifest. It is a form of surrendering to a higher consciousness in which I acknowledge and declare is God because there have been many people following systems, people, traditions, religions, money and idols that we thought was the right way. There is a way that seem right to humans that sometimes lead to destruction.

    We make decisions from our thoughts. Our thoughts dictate our decision-making process. We have the ability to make decisions but do not have the will. God has a will and only God has the ability to operate according to his will. Now is the time to consider our own ways, still being of the mindset of loving ourselves no matter where we are at in life. I once heard a preacher say "Love yourself where you are, but love yourself enough not to stay there." Be reminded; a chess match with yourself have to be won by the more aggressive you.

    Please let us consider this; could most of our contentions come as a result of the patterns we have formulated as a prerequisite to our mindsets of confusion and double mindsets. Let us watch and be mindful of the patterns we are forming throughout our lives in reference to patterns in our relationships, in the way we handle finances, and how we destroy or bodies. Let us begin to change our patterns.

Increase, growth, abundant life, progression, and joy come from movement. No movement = Death. We are designed to consistently move in order to experience positive increase in our health, mindset, finances, and what so ever our heart desire. One of the most critical reasons most us are frustrated, lacking, depressed, discouraged, and experiencing no growth in areas of our personal lives, our ministry, works, our careers, and businesses is because of little to no movement. We are stagnant, paralyzed, slothful, lazy, and unknowledgeable of truth or have no relationship with Yeshua and this can cause us to be living life only to survive. Another reason why you may not be experiencing growth is due to bad connections or you lack wisdom. Once again no movement = no growth, lack, poverty, no increase, no peace, no joy, no hope, no success, and no abundant life.

It is time to allow God to transform us into His image. As Bishop T.D. Jakes quoted, "It is not for God alone that I chase Him. He has the secret to my potential and I had to chase Him to find out who I was." The key to me is within me. The now me is not the only or final me even when I open up to the better evolved me on the next level. It will not be the existent evolved me on the level after that. In God, we are infinite beings forever progressing. Know that in God forever on this earth, you will progress, move forward to, expand and grown into a more advanced you. By the time you finish reading this book, at the end you will be validated and assured with more and more peace within. Read on please, in order to be conformed into the next chapter in your life.

Unit Reflection 7

If you unclothe your façade, do you believe people would be accepting of the real you, why or why not?

Will YOU Allow the Real Me to Come Forth?

We have a choice to be just about whoever we would like to be, but what about being who God made us to be? Some may say God made me like this or I was born like this: only one of these conclusions is right. Yes, we were born like this; but God has nothing to do with us coming out of our mother's womb not being whole and of sound body and mind. That is exactly why there was a miracle performed by Yeshua referenced in the Bible where he healed the child that was born blind and he changed the child from the condition he was born in initially blind into being able to see.

 Some of us think because we were born a certain way it was because God cursed us, our parents sinned, or either it could be a possibility our birth was a mistake. This is not truth; this mindset comes from the intellect of humans. No one is born raciest, a murderer, a liar, a theft, ignorant etc. These are learned behaviors, but we can renew our mindsets. We have to come to ourselves meaning coming into our right minds.

 Referencing Luke 15:11-32 in the Bible, there is a similar depiction of the prodigal son, a boy that left his father's house, took his inheritance and ventured out to doing things that were detrimental to his wellbeing. The prodigal son eventually came to himself; his true self, his right mind. Sometimes it takes some of us going through some challenging oppositions in order for us to realize why we are in a place, physically and mentally that is not conducive to our wellbeing or wellbeing of others; then coming to understand that there has to be a better life for me.

Listen, coming into your true self and identity does not mean we will never have any more problems, test or trails because we surely will. As long as we are on this earth, we will have to deal with humans, which may not have yet arrived to be their true selves. There will always be some form of opposition. I am just acknowledging that it will not stop us from moving forward in peace assurance and victory. Others may oppose us but we will not allow their oppositions to dictate how we act and how we feel.

Within the Bible scriptures it shares with us that opposition took Jeremiah, Moses, Peter, Joshua and many other people of God through a series of ups and down mentally. I do believe this book would have helped them through their journey a little better. These men of God did not go through their frustration because they did not know who they were. Oh yes, they walked in their truthful identity but what they contended with was to be examples to better us on our journey.

Do not miss the opportunity of change that is being revealed to you on this day. Awaken from sleep to a tranquil exuberance and come into enthusiasm to promote hope unto one person, it maybe by you sharing a smile, good day, or a small good deed. Every day is an opportunity for you to improve yourself for the better. What you respect is what you will attract. We respect healing but we do not respect good health. Who and what you do not respect as in having any regard to will move away from you.

Just know you are the one and the only sure candidate to break out of what Sophia Stewart and I agree with as the Matrix effect. I believe because you are reading this book solidifies you are predestined to break the cycle of negativity, lack, falseness, and destruction of life. Yes, you continue to persist to pursue the true essence of your being. Please do not be slumbered into a revolving circle remember: no change no change. It is insanity to believe that if we continue to do the same thing repeatedly, change will come.

You are an important soul on earth with purpose. Walking in who you are really supposed to be will free you up from walking in jealousy, envy, hatred, and strife towards anybody. God is reinventing us unto our original design and purpose. Consciousness awareness = the rising of day = light. Are you really who you have been projecting? If not I suggest that, you awaken into a new period of life. We should not define our world by troubles, lack, hurts, and hatred. Troubles do not make us or break us. Our eyes opening to truth frees us up to our true self and that is why we can experience peace in the midst of trouble.

You are the one that will not be a part of this world's cycle of advancement, meaning success is determined by the third generation. Know you will do and obtain the Kingdom of God principles, which will assist you in being the person who will store up an inheritance for three generations down. You are blessed to be a blessing this is the real you. Just understand I am not referring to careers, jobs, or training. I am referring to your divine purpose of the heart that promotes compassion and help for others.

There are four types of people on any continent: a giver, a taker, a faker, and a maker. Which will we be in the process of time? Our careers, professions, and titles are not the real us. It is just jobs according to and dictated by the world system, which is validation. We may love what we do in our area of expertise, but it is still not who we are. We are compassionate givers, makers, and helpers of our fellowman. Continue reading with joy I will converse with you through the identity points in the back of the book. Read on. It is on now. Are you ready to walk in your truth?

Unit Reflection 8

Make a list of some factors that you know may hinder your progression of allowing the real you to come forth.

Obtaining Oneness within Ourselves

The true defining factor that has promoted, suggested, and persuaded many of us reading this book, is that it is sometimes difficult to be true to ourselves and for us to walk in the true essence of our own being without reserve and discouragement. Most of the time this insight is predicated upon division within ourselves and the divisions amongst each other. God created us all with different personalities, for various purposes as individuals that connects as one in Gods own will, and divine design. God never created anything to not to have a purpose that would benefit something or someone simultaneously even without our knowledge. Everything that is in existence is because God wanted it to exist, which surpasses our ability to comprehend and we mere humans actually do not have to understand all things even though there are some humans that attempt to figure out God by putting God into the box and concepts of the human psyche and intellect. It is ludicrous for any human to believe that they can really know, understand, and figure out an infinite God.

    We humans only understand a tiny concept of the creator God and this statement discredits many of the religious theologian's church beliefs about God. A lot of the doctrine we have been teaching about God comes from the human concepts of what we have learned and believed what is right and wrong. Remember the Bible states God thoughts and ways are far passed our human abilities, ways, thoughts, and knowing's. There are also many scientists and explorers that seem to believe that they have all knowledge of our human existence. Do we really believe this notion when no human has even come close to exploring the trillion of galaxies or even the vast depth of the seas and oceans? Come on everyone let us admit and confess we just do not know all things pertaining to our existence in this life. Nevertheless, there is one thing we should be sure about and that is one creator, God, makes all humans. Yes, even the humans that birth through test tubes and technology in scientific laboratories. Yes, even those life forms only can exist by the breath given to them by creator God.

So, that brings me to this conclusion: since the creator God made everything that is made, all of us humans were obviously made by one God thus solidifying this fact that we all are one in unity. Though, in most cases we as people are only united by contact or geographies we must still on a consistent basis have the mindset of; that we all belong and we all are connected to the one God Creator. As a result, we should know and be okay with the true essence and the true unique identity of each of our existing on this earth. No matter what each other looks like, presents themselves as, and the variety of our purposes each of us have, let us learn to be okay with each other and allow everyone to experience and seek their true identities without us tying to conform them or allowing others to conform us into our small boxes of judging mindsets. Let us start with looking in the mirror again but this time with humility in being okay to receive and see our own reflection as unique sufficient, powerful, and with purposes that God designed. Now we do not have to lie in the mirror, anymore. Now we can integrate our various personalities into the true essence of one being. We have embarked upon an opportunity to pull ourselves together. Continue reading please. There is more that will intrigue you in this effort of you reflecting a true reflection of yourself from this day forward.

Unit Reflection 9

Would you object to other people walking in their true identity no matter their ethnic group, cultural background, sexual preference, gender, weight, physical appearance, religious belief, and financial status? Explain why.

Evolving into the True Essence of Me

There are two elements of understanding that most of the time may dictate our reality on earth in reference to our identities, which are the matrix and MK-Ultra. The matrix factor is produced by systems and ideologies from some leaders, scientists, government officials, private organizations, and cultural upbringing including most religious views. Listed are a just a few of the systems and ideologies that I believe are concealing, and assist in the process of dumbing some us humans down from the truth about our existence on the planet. I also believe this is an extension of MK-Ultra; the CIA's mind control project, which is a predictive modeling to test human response before the actual planned event. In other words, MK-Ultra shows and tells what will happen before it manifests with the effort in mind to desensitize human's rational thinking process. This information is in the United States of America archives; this information is for public review (open, unclassified document). In addition, MK-Ultra is presented virtually through and by media, news, movies, books, and music owned by huge companies.

    We must learn to be consciously aware of what is being promulgated to use. "How?" you may ask. Consider being open-minded and learn how to view situations from a broader perspective. It is important not to be idol in your ability to think outside the box in regards to the ideologies of religion and worldly concepts. You can learn to think outside the box by continual research and knowledge. In doing so I believe, people will be prompt to know the difference between authenticity and facades or false information about themselves from a personal standpoint.

You may be asking how you will truly know the authenticity level of what you are being shown and told. Authenticity depends on the level of peace you have within yourself. Also, whether or not its efforts is to unify or ostracize some humans or maybe even put some people against other people by race, ethnic groups, size, age, gender looks, status, religious beliefs and financial status. Listen we must come to the knowledge; that in this season of your life and mines there will be a shifting of information that we will have access to, that will most surely move us to another level of realizing who we humans are and who we are evolving to.

This book is just one of the catalysts in awakening your conscious awareness to such events as of the truth about our identities. Question: Are not you frustrated in not knowing your true identity? If your answer is yes, this book is for you assisting you in this endeavor of seeking true essence of your identity. Just know that there is a whole truth about your identity and my identity and obviously, our personal mirrors have not been revealing the whole truth about how we see ourselves. If you and I were honest with ourselves our lives in a quest to find whom the true us is and has been somewhat like a chess game. We continue to keep moving all over the chess board with the confused mindset that we are being strategic intellectually in our adjustment in our moves in which most of the time leads to despair and with some even death.

    This is why I do not agree or coincide with the statement suggested by a great well-known writer that wrote, "It does not matter if we humans never understand the truth about our personal existence or identity." The gist of this writer's statement is saying just go with the flow. I believe you would beg to differ as well because you and I have a God-given right to know really, who we are and why we exist. Could it be that we have an inquiring mindset and even a desire within us to know the whole truth and nothing but the truth so help us, God?

If so, we must exemplify extreme caution, especially when associating with other people whether it is our family, associates, coworkers, friends, church leaders and parishioners, and especially the politicians. Some people in our lives have the potential and motives to hinder us from obtaining the truth about us and our purposes in this world. Those people can hinder you by you not guarding your mind and heart and allowing their influence, prestige, money, and power of suggestion to dictate how you act, what you believe and how you respond to reality and truths about your identity.

I am learning this through the events situations and opportunities in my own personal life. For example, I enjoy going to events and places by myself but there are sometimes I would rather connect and fellowship with others through visits and outings. However, I had an experience in connecting and going out with a group of churchgoers and a couple of friends that entailed a bad experience for me; to the level of discard they were sharing towards other churchgoers. I heard a lot of negativity in reference to others that they once fellowshipped with in church in the past. I experienced lack of compassion coming from their character in reference to helping their fellow humans also the divisiveness and malice of for thought towards even one of their neighbors. It ruined the remainder of my day until the next morning because I expected more from them. I expected them to have the same level of compassion as me and I expected them to forgive as I had even in cases of people hurting me.

    I guess I had too high of expectation for the people I was going out with on that particular day when they did not meet my measure of apathy, love and consideration. I allowed how they were acting to cause and prompt me to judge and look at them from a negative connotative. In which making me just as wrong as I perceived them. In most cases, some of us mimic other people negative behaviors, language, beliefs, and habits that are in our company.

Be careful, you know that is not the real true essence of your heart. That is why I am making you aware to be careful and mindful of who you connect with and how you perceive them and their actions because their ways can become your ways; thus, having you and I to take delight in the company of some people that could possibly cause and persuade us to be conformed to their mindsets. The day after I experienced this behavior of judging others, negatively I had an epiphany; it was just as God was impressing on my heart that I was not acting in my true identity. I do not know about you but the closer I move towards the essence personal admiration also the knowledge of God; the more aware I am on how I should treat others and how I should handle situations whether it be good or bad. See I told you; we would see even more better in the mirror now.

Unit Reflection 10

Do you think you can be at peace with yourself, walking in another identity opposite from the one you operated as a year ago?

Changing Mirrors

Thus far; after subjectively reading this book with I am sure with an open mind, our thoughts have been provoked to now understand and perceive this spiritual enlightenment and conclusion of the whole matter on who could we as an individual consider ourselves as being from a true sense of existing in this worlds eyes. Are we really convinced; that who we see in the mirror, is a true sense of our identity? Is the person we see in the mirror; a conformity, product, puppet or maybe a continuation of who we will eventually become in this life journey. You do realize we are evolving progressively and growing into wisdom, knowledge, and comprehension whether that is psychically, spiritually and psychologically. We are expanding sociably, physically and mentally. Let's make it happen for the good.

Listen; I am not trying to contradict the previous writings in this book, in reference to we possibly being conformed by others, our surroundings, our motives, self- awareness, and also our instructive behaviors. I am saying but not with the resolve, but with humbleness of mind, truth and reality. We all at any given moment in time; transform, conform, appear and digress into whoever we desire the mirror to show in order to cohabitate in this world.

In other words, we operate according to the times, conditions, and situations at hand. Does this mean we are not walking in our true identity? No! This means we often walk, as we believe we should at that precise given time. Question: Do we ever and will we ever be and walk in our true identity and will the mirror stop lying? No, it is impossible to walk in our true identity in this world except we be transformed by God, redeveloping our minds to see and think like He instructs us to, from a kingdom of God prospective.

Allow me to elaborate in depth. From the time conception and even before we as embryos are being programmed by our parents, who use different sounds as music, reading, loud talking, whether negative or positive even submerging themselves under water in order to mold their babies, after birth the parent make choices for us and promulgate their agenda, beliefs and dysfunctions into the babies' minds, even what types of food eaten. It actually takes years before the growing child can make decisions on its own, decisions steaming from whatever they have adapted to during their early stages of life; such as picked up habits and traits that will eventually be difficult to break. Remember the brain stores information. The information passed down from generation to generation affects us in ways that can dictate our personalities for years.

This process of changing from a lying mirror is just that a process and in this book, I have shared information that has aroused your attention, giving us all a fair opportunity to work ourselves from a constructive point of view as a work in progress, a work unfinished. But with the will to do better and progress in desired areas of our life, by receiving and understanding some truths about us that most of us have avoided to face for years. But today is a good place to start. We all must acknowledge, by now we have been expressing different identities in our mirrors; sometimes a Joker, sometimes a King, sometimes a Queen and most of the time confused.

Listen, it will not be any easy transformation from confusion of identities toward liberty in who we really are. Allow me to give some examples; some of us are stuck in a façade (lying mirror) with marriage, careers, jobs, education, relationships, business agreements, associates, religion, church, affiliation and etc. Most of us are connected to people and things that you are having to pretend and what makes it difficult is the fact that you are stuck and seemly, there is no way out and there is no hope of ever being honest about it and to be liberalized from it. However, there is still a system of hope that this book has established.

Be reminded of the following:
A. It is a choice.
B. It is a decision to do or not do.
C. You have to trust your decision.
D. Understand no one will accept your choice of moving forward
E. It may take time for you to have peace in your decision to move on towards your new identity.
F. Eventually you will experience peace, joy, assurance, and victory, knowing you are free to be the true essence of who God ordained you to be.

Paul an apostle of Yeshua stated it so profoundly

in Biblical Scripture like this: I was all things to all because I have a purpose. Paul's true identity was his God given purpose and that was to gain others to Christ. Final question for you: What is your purpose in who you are seeing in the mirror? First, we all have many purposes and when we realize our true purposes, then we will finally see and experience a true mirror, which will not happen overnight.

I will not say what your true identities are, but I will note for the record that whoever and whatever you are really supposed to be on this earth, if it is to be your true identity, revolves around and with the God kind of love (unconditionally helping others) for all.

Remember, do not be discouraged and frustrated when others cannot see past what and who they suppose your only purpose is on this earth. Nevertheless, be encouraged to go forward, stand still, experience, and promulgate the many other purposes yet pondered on because we are bigger than we expect. Just let it be big and with and by Gods love.

Now you and I are in a better place and mindset to be productive citizens in this world amongst the wolves.

Once you begin to activate your purposes, you may develop characteristics similar to a giver, carrier of hope, or become a gift to a world full of hopelessness. Therefore, I encourage you to try hard to be the best you; you can be in order for you to walk in peace, assurance, and victory in the essence of helping others on a positive note because God designed us to need each other's existence.

    You are too valuable, you have worth, and you are significant. We have not and you have not seen the best reflection of you yet, but we all will sooner than later as you continue to seek to experience your true identity. Happiness is waiting for you only because you are a gift. We look forward to observing the mirror you are going to reflect to us by helping our world in this next chapter of your liberalized life. Now read on.

Pretending to be Okay

Before I start, allow me to share to you: IT IS OKAY TO TELL. Living in the beautiful world can be at times very difficult mentally for most of us humans. Many of us tend to live a secluded and secret life that even inadvertently, subject us to many associates, coworkers, constituents, comrades, family, friends, classmates and religious sects. But needless to say, we are still lonely. It has been stated by many we can be in a room with a lot of people, laughing and conversing but we as individuals are still living with a sense of being all alone, which puts us in a mindset of being sometimes afraid of sharing our inner most struggles. Many of us are crying aloud within ourselves, but no one else can hear us. We do not feel we can tell anyone our truths, hurts, pains and struggles because most of us believe we would be frowned upon. We may also feel as if no one cares anyways.

However, after reading this book thus far it could be a fact that most of us are afraid to just be who we are. Therefore, we tend to continue in the difference facades, in order not to be rejected but accepted as being this strong, focused, knowledgeable, sweet, innocent, sound person that should be honored and respected. This is a very dangerous façade or masquerade to promulgate. It is why many suffer with mental illness, depression, loneliness, confusion, suicidal thoughts and misery without treatment and assistance. It is so very dangerous to keep so much hurt to ourselves and it could be very damaging living in a world desiring help but pretending we do not need it. I label this "secret pain." Now is the time to talk and express to someone other than yourself your struggles with the hope of at minimum having them to be a listening ear.

Be reminded we all, as human, experience approximately 7000 thoughts a day and we all know that all of those 7000 thoughts are not positive. We really need to deal with our issues with each other. I believe it would defiantly help this to happen when more of us humans begin to be transparent, share, and express more love towards one another. By humbling ourselves and by being empathetic toward each other situations without being judgmental. I ask you this day. Are you apart of the problem (not caring and being judgmental), or maybe are you apart of the solution (compassionate and understanding)? I pray we all are the latter.

It is time to face and confront our lying mirrors of pretending we are okay. Because attempting to ignore the issues we have; the secret issues can contribute to abuse of drugs, alcohol, sexual perversions, gambling, and staying in seclusion, which only cover up and sooth the situations for a short period of time and can never take the pain away permanently. I come to realize, the main reason we are hesitant to reach out and open up to others and we rather chose to continue to live a lie is only because everyone of us humans are starving for true love. The Bible describes this type of unconditional love as "Agape" God's type of love. If and when we humans allow this love to move through people, then and only then, will begin our liberty and peace towards one another without fear and judging. We then can stop faking, we then can stop lying, we then can stop dying slowly from the lack of love.

Oh, when we as individuals begin our quests to humble ourselves and accept our true identities without reserve not being overly concerned about the negativity coming from others but let us start be realizing this as well; there has been studies done that shows; there are tragic events that happened to us in our adolescent days that contributes in molding our psyche (the center of thought, feeling, and motivation consciously and unconsciously directing the body's reactions to its social environment). All this means; there may be somethings that happened to us that we have suppressed when we were young and unknowingly developed into traits and behaviors that moves us to act in certain ways or cause us to express openly a reflection in the mirror that is not the true essence of our being. Some call it; cause and effect. Now we must, by reading this book realize this, maybe cause and effect is the contribution to our actions in the present images we project. Once we understand this, we then can begin the process of changing from some of the attributes of our past negative or tragic experiences, that influenced us to act unseemly.

Most of us need counseling but never are administered help or an opportunity to open up and share. Just know, it was not your fault and it is not all of your fault that you act negatively now. However, if after reading this book you do not submit to change or attempt to find out how to face change: you walking negatively will be your fault. We all must admit it is time to work on ourselves to seek changing into our true image of love, patience, humor, respect, temperance, joy, peace, and being empathetic towards others and then we can enjoy happiness in this life even amongst chaotic situations. In addition, thus being able to look in the mirror of our life and be comfortable and pleased with who we are as an individual has become. Are you really ready to embark upon this journey a long with me and numbers of others to choose to be true to themselves and everyone else no matter what? Say Yes!

On a Quest to Understand

This may be the beginning of some of our quest to understand and put at rest our own identity crises. The main objective for writing this book was to assist in the process of awakening the conscious awareness within one self to come to the realization that we as individuals are unique in our own precepts and concepts on our level of intellectual understandings about ourselves as persons who are designed only by God. In which, God is the supreme entity; for God is the creator of purpose for us in this life and beyond. In which we all should come to a place in each of our mindsets of peace, surety, hope, love for ourselves and all others. In order to experience a peace of mind and tranquility to the best of our ability by consistently reflecting on the personal encounters with God by the events of life, by individuals we connect with on life's journey and by what we experience in any given moment. This is continually evolving into who we already were from the beginning of existence before our earthly experience.

    I have come to understand that the majority of us humans are not mentally operating at full capacity in thought, due to the fact that part of our human brains are lying dormant. The systems of this world are putting a lot of effort in keeping our minds locked into the functioning of brain dormancy by feeding our left-brain, also known as the left hemisphere with constant information that caters to our ego. The right side of the brain also known as the right hemisphere is most likely completely shut down which is causing majority of the human race to experience and understand their lives from the lowest common denominator of consciousness. When the right side of the brain is dormant it limits one's ability to comprehend who they really supposed to be and how to operate on this planet and beyond; this is why so many of us in the human race discover and operate in the mindset of frustration, confusion, stress, and bondage.

God wants us free and we can experience even more liberty mentally if we learn to use more of the right side of our brain. Learning to use the right hemisphere of the brain can allow one to experience and advance in the level of knowledge and truth from a more 3 dimensional or spiritual unseen realm. Please do not confuse spirituality with religious or traditional concepts. Experiencing spirituality in an unseen realm it exists for our expansion and mental advancement into more abundance of life and God's awesome glory and essence of love, joy, peace, and power. In addition, we become eligible and more comfortable to implement new ideas and encounter more advanced options of living life on a higher level beyond our current thoughts, heart desires, hopes, and dreams.

As mentioned in the previous chapters of this book we are coming out of what some of us call "The Matrix Effect" which means being controlled and programmed by the framework of organizations with diabolical motives in which they feed the left side of our brain by using the media, government politics, religion, propaganda etc. Ian R. Crane stated that our left-brain hemisphere is hormonally retarded. According to Ian, our left-brain hemisphere is perceptually limited and a cognitively impaired version of our right-brain hemisphere and our left-brain hemisphere is perceptually dominant and it defines who we are and usually decides who we think we are. Let us not continue to allow the left-brain hemisphere (our ego) to continue adhering to programming and dictating who we are. Let's all begin a quest to seek out who we already are and lets be okay with exploring the notion that there's definitely more to we as individuals, than we have been programmed to believe.

Just know despite how the matrix attempts to influence how we govern ourselves, be mindful we all are capable and responsible for enhancing our brains by being open to instruction and knowledge that will reopen the right hemisphere of our brain to enhance our overall functioning. Due to you reading this book, most likely you are more enlightened to the truth, you do have a true identity and every day you are given the opportunity to seek and determine who you want to be and not put your primary focus on how other people perceive you to be now. Be excited to know that there is a more advanced version of you that's been presented. This quote from the Holy Bible is one of my favorites 1st Corinthians 2:9 – 14 (KJV);

9   But as it is written, Eye have not seen, nor ear heard, neither have entered into the heart of human kind, the things which God hath prepared for them that love him.

10   But God hath revealed them unto us by his Spirit: for the Spirit searcheth all things, yea, the deep things of God.

11   For what person knoweth the things of a man, save the spirit of man which is in him (the right brain hemisphere)? even so the things of God knoweth no man, but the Spirit of God.

12   Now we have received, not the spirit of the world (matrix, left-brain hemisphere), but the spirit which is of God (the supreme); that we (humankind) might know the things that are freely given to us of God.

13   Which things also we speak, not in the words which man's wisdom teacheth, but which the Holy Ghost teacheth; comparing spiritual things with spiritual.

14   But the natural person (the programmed person) receiveth not the things of the Spirit of God: for they are foolishness unto that person (who's mind is limited): neither can that person know them, (the new spiritual insight) because they are spiritually discerned.

I know I sound like a gospel preacher but it is only because that's one of my God given purposes on this planet at this season in earthly time. I am more excited this day as you to know that there is more to us than meets the eye. So, let us not focus on a primary purpose on this earth because we all have many purposes, let us just continue to seek out who we are and who we were in the beginning of existence by the mind of the Supreme Being who most of us label as God. Remember we humankind are infinite beings not mere finite beings.

The Authors Final Answer & Conclusion

Okay I have shared, you have received, now we understand, the process and decision we all have to give effort to in order to experience peace, assurance and liberty to be who we are without reserve and to walk in the true essence of our real identities, but having God's wisdom on how. Do not forger this transition from Lying Mirrors to your True Identities will not come easy because most of us humans are more concerned about having things than about becoming and being true to ourselves by pulling greatness out that lies within us. Know that there is more chapters to your life, and it is time to time to move forward towards the new chapters by not holding on to the previous chapters.

This book will be a key tool for us to use in our efforts to be free enough not to present to others Lying Mirrors (falsehoods, pretending to be someone we are not). This book prompt us all to be broad minded and to expand our consciousness and awareness about ourselves and the established systems of this world, that tries to dictate who are as humans are to be by dumbing us down with falsehoods and lies about who we are. We now believe; we do not have to emulate others in order to be accepted in this society. We realize our true identities are right before us and within us and because we are consciously aware we now know that we as individuals have power to experience a happier, fulfilling existence on this earth, if we choose.

This book Lying Mirrors has and will continue to inspire us on a personal level and as any instructional manual towards opening ourselves up to new and great possibilities by first acknowledging there is a true person (inner self) that needs embracing. It is the divine part of us, that encourage, each of us that it is important to become free from self-destructive tendencies we allow and to begin to pull on and operate in the beautiful journey of becoming liberalized from the confusion of our identities.

Always be reminded:

A. We all have more than one purpose in this life. We have many and we have been operating in those various purposes all of our lives.

B. Being stagnant and stuck is a choice to resist nature and to resist God's will for our life.

C. We all evolve, expand, and grow its inevitable. So, let's work along with growth and improvement for the betterment of our lives.

D. Knowledge and learning is handed down through time, let us acquire more knowledge and expand our consciousness about our existence in this God given gift of Life.

E. It's been stated by neuroscientist for years; humans only use 10 to 13 percent of our brains. So, we all should consider to stop thinking we know it all and everyone else is wrong, especially the beautiful religious folk from all over this world. Do not count us all out, you only know a little as the rest of us humans. Even your Bible shares; "That there are many other things which The Christ did, that if they should be written, even the world itself could not contain all the books. So, please do not be counted amongst the number of people that curse and count people out that do not have the same belief as you do.

Let us all be opened minded considerate, empathetic and compassionate, towards all because the ultimate charge on your life now is to work on yourself first and consider your ways, whether or not you are observing a mirror full of lies, pretending and confusion.

IT IS NOT THE REAL YOU!

God speed on your new endeavor of realizing your true essence and your real identities.

Peace, Blessings, and Love.

Let's All Strive To Be The Best Version Of Our True Selves!

Consequences of Walking in Lying Mirrors

When we Siblings, when we Brothers, when we Sisters, when we Husbands, when we Co-Workers, when we Paramours, when we Leaders, when we Friends, when we Associates, when we Pastors and Ministers of any religious affiliation, when we Parents, when we Sons and Daughters of our biological parents, when we Teachers, when we Police, when we City & State Officials, when we Business Owners, when we Caretakers, when we Politicians, when we Neighbors and when we other Humans; operate in a façade, what this book calls a falsehood, a pretend lifestyle, we can cause known and unknown let downs and discouragement within the people associated with us and our fantasy lives, when the truth about us is revealed.

Lying to others about who we really are can also

cause us the individual to become suicidal, embarrassed, shame, lonely, ostracized bewildered, fearful, stressed, combative, angry, hateful, defensive and may cause us to go into deep depression and seclusion. I am sure we all understand these consequences to be a damaging and unhappy state of affairs, but consequently can be rectified with this book, counseling and God's Grace. We must realize now that being phony is not worth the negative consequences that we may have to endure.

It's been time for all of us to rethink, reevaluate, redo, and reconsider each Lying Mirror we have represented, whether it was a Fake King, Fake Queen, or a Fake Joker. Be reminded there is only one mirror we have we have to look in at time. But many images being projected from one mirror are not good for them that are watching us. So, without any reservation, I believe after reading a book I wrote; that it is way better to just be the best you that you will allow yourself to be.

Identity Points

I. Being embarrassed; meaning to feel awkward, self-conscious or ashamed about something you have done, said or thought in the presence of others, is a choice. You do not have to believe in others opinions to the level of giving any human power over you to make you feel ashamed, all humans have flaws. Stop being ashamed of who you are supposed to be really be.

II. We must be able to distinguish between our nature and our nurturing; in other words, each of us conformed into who we are now because of our upbringing the way our parents and the people we recognize as family raised us by the teaching of their level of knowledge. On the other hand, could it possibly be the nature of our mindset due to a chemical and biological makeup, which contributes to each of our DNA structure? I want you to know that each of us must realize that even though our nature and the way we are all as individuals were nurtured we still have to develop the nerves and courage to be a part of the decision-making process towards our destiny on Earth as we adhere to the true essence of our inner identity.

III. We are like caterpillars, always changing into who we will be but at the same time being who we are. As you consistently evolve choose not be confused or frustrated with yourself in the process. Be okay with being the best you that you can be with peace in the essence of the true you even when other people do not celebrate with in the evolving processes. We do not have to chase purpose and destiny because the two are running us each down.

IV. Please do not allow others to limit or lock you into who you are now, because they do not expect you to do anything other than what you have presented to them as of now. Just know you have more than one purpose and there is always more evolving in your life to come. Because if you allow people to stop and hinder you and your moving more into your true identity, it will frustrate and torment you during your effort to advance towards your individual liberty.

V. Being real and becoming your true self does not require you to share all your personal business to everyone you come in contact with, we should only share personal secrets to those professionals that we choose to administer help to our situations.

VI. It is still possible for other people to pull the greater out of you, therefore do not automatically reject all advice from all people in reference to who they see you to be. Some of the advice provided by other people could be constructive criticism with love and appreciation for a positive outlook on your true identity, future and evolution.

VII. You are not just only who you have been in your past. We have all done some negative things in our lives thus far but whatever we have done in this life does not mean it is who we are. There is more to us there are more personalities we will evolve into eventually throughout our existence. Stop allowing other people to marginalize you by keeping you in a box of whom they consider you to be because of something you already done.

VIII. Do not be accepting of the notions that may attempt to torment your mind in reference to convincing you that there is no hope for change coming to you and that you will stay the way you are at this particular time.

IX. Sometimes we that are seeking our true identities must practice being still and patient, be reminded; no one can see their reflections in moving water but only when water is standing still then we can see our reflections.

X. Make note that change is not easy. Continue to practice and make an effort to continue to evolve into a better you and even when you make a mistake, restart where you are and continue to strive to present the best reflection of you possible.

XI. Just know that the true essence of our being has not yet been tapped into by the human brain or psyche. No human have 100% understood their being in humanity. We are only assuming most of the time who we are. Being too serious about finding your purpose may cause frustration and disenchantment. Just live life to its fullest with love and appreciation.

XII. Always remember your self-worth is not validated by the material things you have obtained, level of wealth you seek, or by your status amongst your associates. Because things that we can obtain do not establish our true identity, who we can possibly connect with do not solidify who we supposed to be. Our self-worth and truth comes with peace, joy, happiness, love, and serenity within inner being.

XIII. Be okay with yourself in spite of knowing just because you are living in your truth do not mean you will be mistake-free you still will error along the way just continue to move forward towards your destiny.

XIV. Always be reminded to be grateful and humbly thankful of the mere fact that you have life and that you are somebody special, important, and surely loved by God.

XV. Be who you feel comfortable being without reserve and without fear of being rejected by others.

XVI. Make sure your associates and significant others will come in contact with the real you, not some pretender from a reflection of the multiple façade you have projected. There are many marriages ending in divorce because the people who they married were not true in their real identity.

XVII. Why do you spend so much mental bliss trying to hide who you really are and attempting to be someone who you are not; is it because you do not want people to know or see who you really are? Stop, calm down, listen to your heart and what your heart is telling you that will make for peace in your now; no matter who you are in the company of. Just let your guard down and present the true you of what you really desire to express which promote peace and serenity for yourself and others in your company by knowing and being okay with who you are. Being fake is not an option.

XVIII. This point starts with a question; why are so many of us humans confused about our true identities? Well that is my point (the word identities) we have to understand that we all evolve and grow daily and yearly this prompting us all to experience life from many different aspects. In most cases like this causes us to conform to not only our growth and knowledge and different experiences, but in the growth we all advanced intellectually in where we fit for that particular time in life. Meaning we can be for one thing at a particular time in history but change in that same thing or mindset in another time in the future. This does not mean we are flip-flopping; but we look at things different in the evolution of life. Be okay with change throughout your life. Change for the better. Just like a caterpillar who starts out as a cocoon (it's true identity at that point in time) then a caterpillar (its true identity at that point in time) then it becomes or evolve into a butterfly (it's true identity at that point in time).

XIX. Never cease trying to break the code of your True Identity that's where peace lies. This world tends to prevent most people from ever walking in the real essence of their true identity.

Afterword

Remember all of us humans are in development on this life's journey and I heard someone say development begins when we receive an inclination of who we might be and then we proceeding to achieve clarity and even eventually more and more clarity of our real identities. Therefore, we must go forward in adhering to the quest to grasp onto and even advance through our evolving as conscious beings to even greater heights of acknowledging who we will be after a while. Journey with me in our quest to experience presenting the real reflection of us to others as long as we exist.

    Can you just imagine for a few minutes how better off the humans of the world could be if only more of us discovered who we were in reference to our true identity? Our life would not have to be so confusing or a chess game anymore. Thank you for experiencing this enlightenment through the words and inspiration of this book. I now expect you to ride out the progression of your personal journey with me in our quest to experience presenting the real reflection of us to others as long as we exist.

My motive has been throughout the pages of this book is to put the rights and privileges back into your hands in reference to you being the controller and dictator of your image. I hope you accept the challenge to begin the process of evolving into the authentic essence of you.

About the Author

Carter M. Head is a life coach, a minister, and is one of the most dynamic, realistic, and sought-out conference speakers. Carter is a graduate of Andersonville Theological Seminary and Alumni of West Georgia College. Carter founded and established many outreach organizations in reference to feeding and clothing the indigent. Carter also established the YL2 (Youth Leadership League of Henry County, GA), and he coproduced three live stage plays emphasizing on the issues of our youth. Carter established the mentoring group called B.I.N.O. In addition, Carter is an author, grant writer, marriage counselor, and philanthropist.

Other Books by the Author

- ◊ Am I Trump?
- ◊ Unity for What?
- ◊ Questions with No Answers

Made in the USA
Columbia, SC
03 October 2018